Sense and Sensibility

JANE AUSTEN

Level 3

Retold by Cherry Gilchrist
Series Editors: Andy Hopkins and Jocelyn Potter

Pearson Education Limited
Edinburgh Gate, Harlow,
Essex CM20 2JE, England
and Associated Companies throughout the world.

ISBN 0 582 41689 2

First published 1811
This adaptation first published by Penguin Books 1997
Published by Addison Wesley Longman Limited and Penguin Books Ltd. 1998
New edition first published 1999

Typeset by RefineCatch Limited, Bungay, Suffolk
Set in 11/14pt Monotype Bembo
Printed in Spain by Mateu Cromo, S.A. Pinto (Madrid)

Published by Pearson Education Limited in association with
Penguin Books Ltd., both companies being subsidiaries of Pearson Plc

For a complete list of the titles available in the Penguin Readers series please write to your local
Pearson Education office or to: Marketing Department, Penguin Longman Publishing,
5 Bentinck Street, London W1M 5RN.

Contents

Introduction

Marianne forgot about Colonel Brandon, but he did not forget about her. Elinor liked him and was sorry for him, but what could she do? Can a quiet gentleman of thirty-five win against a handsome young one of twenty-five?

Mrs Dashwood and her daughters must leave Norland, their family home, and move to a small house in another part of the country. They have very little money now and must live more simply. But almost at once, Marianne, the middle daughter, meets a handsome young stranger called Willoughby. Soon everybody thinks that they will marry. Elinor, her older sister, is more serious. She loves a quiet, sensible young man called Edward Ferrars. But Willoughby suddenly leaves for London, and Edward doesn't seem interested in Elinor now. What has gone wrong?

Jane Austen, one of England's greatest novelists, was born in 1775 in Hampshire, in the south of England. Her father was a priest and she had eight brothers and sisters. Her greatest friend was her sister, Cassandra, who was two years older. Later, the family moved to the fashionable town of Bath. People came to Bath to drink the waters for their illnesses and to find husbands for their daughters. Jane didn't enjoy Bath very much; she was pleased to move back to Hampshire in 1809.

Jane's family was a loving one and made the most of the parties, dinners and dances that took place in the country. Jane received several offers of marriage but did not accept any of them. She lived quietly and spent much of her time writing. *Sense and Sensibility* (1811) was her first successful book. Next came *Pride and Prejudice* (1813). Jane wrote both these books some fifteen years before they appeared for sale. Two more books followed: *Mansfield Park* (1814) and *Emma* (1816). After her death, two other works, *Northanger Abbey* and *Persuasion* came out.

Jane Austen died in Winchester at the early age of forty-two.

Jane Austen's books describe, with a quiet but sharp sense of fun, a world she knew well: middle-class families with daughters in need of husbands. The perfect husband is young and handsome, loves music and literature, and is good at dancing. More importantly, he has plenty of money and a fine country house. Each book describes the dance of love between young ladies and gentlemen. The wars in Europe at that time do not enter the picture. All attention is on the game of love – a much more serious business.

A film of *Sense and Sensibility* was made in 1996, with Emma Thompson, Kate Winslet and Hugh Grant in the main parts. Other stories by Jane Austen in Penguin Readers are *Pride and Prejudice*, *Emma* and *Persuasion*.

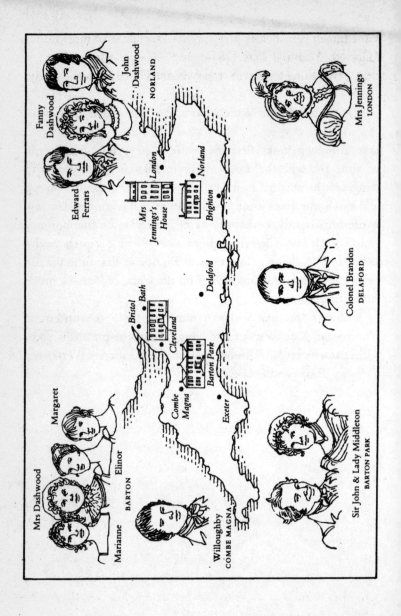

Chapter 1 A New Home

'I'd like to help my sisters,' said John Dashwood. 'My father asked me to do something for them, so I shall give them some money.'

'Oh, but your father was ill!' Fanny, his wife, answered. 'He didn't mean it!'

'But I promised! They need my help.'

His father was dead now and everything was changing in the family. John was the son of Mr Dashwood's first wife; he had plenty of money from his mother, and Fanny was also quite rich. But Mr Dashwood did not have much to give his next wife and their three daughters.

'Well – perhaps we can give them a present,' said Fanny.

'A small present of money – that's a good idea. You're right!' said John.

'No, not money. First, help them to find a new home. And then later send them some fruit, or fish, or meat. Why do they need money? They can live very cheaply!'

'Of course! Yes, that's what my father wanted,' John decided happily. He was not a bad man, but he listened to his selfish wife too much.

Mrs Dashwood and her three daughters – Elinor, Marianne and Margaret – would soon have to leave their family home. This large house, called Norland Park, now belonged to John and Fanny. Mrs Dashwood disliked Fanny, and wanted to leave immediately, but Elinor advised her not to. Elinor was nineteen, and very sensible. She thought carefully about everything. Her mother wanted to move to another large house, but they had to find somewhere cheap.

And so they stayed at Norland for a few more months, living

like visitors in their old home. Fanny's brother, Edward, was also staying there. He was not handsome, but he was a pleasant, clever young man. He and Elinor were often together, and were soon good friends. Mrs Dashwood noticed this.

'In a few months,' Mrs Dashwood said to Marianne, 'Elinor and Edward will get married! Elinor will be so happy!'

'But what shall we do without her?' Marianne asked.

'We'll see her often! But you look sad, Marianne. Don't you like Edward?'

A quiet, serious person like Edward was boring to Marianne. 'Oh, he's a kind man. But he doesn't seem to feel strongly about books and music, or Elinor's beautiful pictures! I must have a different kind of man! But will I ever find one?'

'My dear girl, you're only sixteen!' Mrs Dashwood replied.

In fact, Elinor did like Edward very much. But his sister, Fanny, did not like seeing them together. She and her mother, Mrs Ferrars, wanted a rich wife for Edward, not a poor one like Elinor.

Fanny was rude to Mrs Dashwood about this, 'He is not free for *any* young lady, you know. My mother has special plans for him.'

Mrs Dashwood could not wait to leave Norland.

She was lucky. A letter arrived from Sir John Middleton, a relative from Devon, in the west of England. He wanted to offer her a house not far from his large house, Barton Park. It was a friendly letter and they agreed to move there. The new house was cheap and they could live there easily. Mrs Dashwood still hoped for some money from John, but he did not give them anything. They sold their horses and carriage, and only took three servants with them. 'Dear, dear Norland!' cried Marianne. 'Perhaps I shall never see you again! And oh, you beautiful trees! When shall I walk under your leaves again?'

'He is not free for any *young lady, you know.*'

Chapter 2   An Invitation to Dinner

It was a long way to Devon. But it was a very pretty part of the country, with high hills, fine trees, and open farmland. Their new home had two sitting-rooms and four bedrooms, and was quite comfortable. They put Marianne's piano in one of the sitting-rooms, and some of Elinor's pictures on the walls.

'It's too small,' Mrs Dashwood said, 'but I'll save some money and build more rooms.'

The next day, after breakfast, Sir John Middleton came over to see them. He was about forty, and seemed to be a naturally happy, friendly man. He invited them to dinner at Barton Park, and later sent them some fruit and vegetables from the garden.

Barton Park was a large, handsome house with plenty of servants, about half a mile from their new home. Sir John nearly always had visitors there, and often gave dances too. He liked people, and Lady Middleton liked to serve beautiful meals. But she was a cold woman, who did not say much.

At dinner, they met Mrs Jennings, the mother of Lady Middleton. She was very different from her daughter – a large, happy woman, who talked a lot, and liked to laugh loudly.

'Did you two girls leave your hearts at Norland?' she asked Elinor and Marianne. Both Mrs Jennings's daughters were married, and so she now wanted to marry off the rest of the world! 'Oh, your faces are red,' she laughed.

The other visitor at Barton Park that evening, was a quiet man of about thirty-five. His name was Colonel Brandon and he was a friend of Sir John's. He had a sensible face; he was not handsome, but he was a gentleman.

After dinner, Marianne played the piano and sang, and he was the only person who really listened. Everybody enjoyed the music, but Sir John talked all the time, and Lady Middleton was only interested in her four noisy children. They came in after dinner, pulled her dress and stopped the conversation.

'Colonel Brandon is old,' thought Marianne, 'but he likes my music.'

'He loves her!' thought Mrs Jennings. And soon she told everybody this.

'What a stupid idea!' Marianne said to her mother later. 'How can he feel anything? He's thirty-five years old – an old man!'

'I'm only forty!' Mrs Dashwood laughed. 'And I'm not ready to die yet!'

'Well, perhaps he's not ready to die. But at his age, he can't know anything about love! He needs a nurse, not a wife!'

Chapter 3   The Handsome Stranger

The Dashwoods were now busy and happy in their new home. The girls often went out walking, and one day Marianne and Margaret decided to climb a high hill together, near the house. It was a beautiful morning when they left, but soon black clouds built up in the sky, and it started to rain very hard. They began to run fast down the hill. Margaret got to the bottom, but Marianne fell and could not get up again.

A gentleman was walking near them with his dog. He saw the accident, and immediately came to help them.

'I've hurt my foot!' Marianne said.

'I can carry you,' he replied, and picked her up from the ground. He carried her down the hill, through the garden and into the house. Elinor and her mother were very surprised to see this young man with Marianne in his arms, but he quickly explained everything.

'I can carry you,' he replied, and picked her up
from the ground.

'Oh thank you, thank you!' Mrs Dashwood said again and again. 'Please sit down!'

'No, I'm too dirty and wet from the rain,' he answered. 'But can I come tomorrow? My name is Willoughby.'

He was a handsome young man, and Mrs Dashwood encouraged him to visit them again. And Marianne quickly forgot about her bad foot.

'Do you know this man Willoughby?' they asked Sir John the next day.

'Willoughby? Is he here again? Yes, he's a good man! He rides a horse well and has a clever little dog! Was the dog with him?'

But they were not interested in his dog.

'Who is he?' asked Elinor. 'Does he live here?'

'No, no – he has a relative here, an old lady. He has a very nice house not too far away, at Combe Magna in Somerset, and will be a good husband for somebody! Be careful Elinor – Marianne has Brandon already. She mustn't catch all the men! Perhaps Willoughby will be just right for you!'

'My daughters do not try to catch men!' Mrs Dashwood said angrily.

'Last Christmas,' Sir John continued, 'I invited him to one of my dances, and he danced from eight in the evening until four in the morning!'

'Did he?' asked Marianne. 'That's the kind of man that I like!'

And Willoughby liked the three Miss Dashwoods. He visited them the next day. The two older sisters were both pretty girls; Marianne was taller than Elinor, and had a specially lovely face with a sweet smile and dark, bright eyes. She was shy at first. Then Willoughby saw the piano and talked about music, and Marianne could not stay silent. After this, he came to the house every day.

Sir John also invited the girls to several dances at Barton Park, and Willoughby and Marianne danced together most of the time. It was a happy time for Marianne, and she did not try to keep her feelings a secret.

'My girls will soon have two good husbands,' Mr Dashwood thought. Marianne forgot about Colonel Brandon, but he did not forget her. Elinor liked him, and was sorry for him, but what could she do? Can a quiet gentleman of thirty-five win against a handsome young one of twenty-five?

One day, there was a plan to visit Whitwell, a fine house with some beautiful gardens. Some friends of Colonel Brandon lived there. Everybody planned to drive there in carriages from Barton Park – the Middletons, the Dashwoods, Colonel Brandon, Willoughby, and a few more friends too. They all arrived at Barton early, and were looking forward to the day's adventure.

But during breakfast, Colonel Brandon came in with a letter. He looked unhappy.

'I'm very sorry,' he said, 'but I must go to London immediately to finish some important business. We can't go to Whitwell today. My friends are away, and the servants don't know you – you won't get in without me.'

This was an unpleasant surprise.

'Well,' Lady Middleton said, 'you'll be back soon, and we'll go to Whitwell then, won't we?'

'Perhaps I won't be able to return. I can't be sure.'

'We can still go out in the carriages,' Sir John said. 'It's a beautiful day.'

Willoughby said quietly to Marianne, 'Some people don't like this kind of happy party, and Brandon is one of them.'

He and Marianne jumped into their carriage and drove away very fast. The others also drove off and did not see Marianne and Willoughby again until much later.

There was a dinner, and a small dance at Barton Park for everyone that evening. Mrs Jennings sat next to Marianne, and Elinor could hear their conversation.

'And so you had a secret adventure this morning! But I know all about it!'

Marianne turned red in the face.

'We went out in my carriage,' Willoughby said quickly.

'Ah, but where to? To Allenham!' Willoughby's old aunt lived in Allenham House, but she was away from home that day. 'To the house that will soon be yours!' She laughed. 'Do you like it, Marianne? It's very big, isn't it?'

Marianne could not speak.

'Is this true?' Elinor asked her later.

'Yes, of course it's true! And why not?'

'You and Willoughby went together to this empty house! Oh, Marianne, that wasn't right!'

'It was the nicest morning that I have ever spent! What's wrong with that?'

'If something is nice, it can still be wrong,' Elinor replied quietly.

Mrs Dashwood soon heard the news. 'They're engaged!' she decided. 'He took her to see her new home!'

But Willoughby and Marianne did not tell them anything.

'Ask them, please, mother,' Elinor said anxiously to Mrs Dashwood. 'Are they really engaged? And why is it a secret?'

'Ask her!' repeated Mrs Dashwood. 'No, I can't! I'm sure Marianne will tell me soon. Perhaps Willoughby's aunt doesn't like Marianne. Perhaps they must keep the engagement secret for a few months.'

'I'm not sure. Maybe there *is* no engagement.'

'But he loves her! You can see that.'

'Yes, I can. But I don't understand – there's something strange about it all.'

A few days later, Mrs Dashwood, Elinor and Margaret were coming home from a visit to Lady Middleton.

'Look!' Margaret said. 'There's Willoughby's carriage outside our door!'

The ladies went inside, and immediately Marianne came out of the sitting-room and ran upstairs to her bedroom. She was crying. Willoughby was still standing in the sitting-room. He looked very serious.

'Is Marianne ill?' Mrs Dashwood asked anxiously.

'No – I hope not. I'm sorry – I'm here to say goodbye.'

'Goodbye? Are you going back to London?'

'Yes, this morning.'

'Well, you'll come back soon!'

'Unhappily, that won't be possible. I only see my aunt once a year.'

'But we can invite you! You're always welcome here!'

'You're very kind,' Willoughby said. 'But – I must go now.'

He climbed into his carriage, and drove away.

Chapter 4   A Secret Engagement

Marianne was very unhappy, but she also enjoyed her sadness a little. She did not sleep, eat or speak much. She cried a lot. She liked to walk round the park and think of Willoughby. She sang the songs that they sang together when he was there. She read again the books that they both enjoyed.

One day, the three sisters were out walking along the road to Barton. A man on a horse was riding towards them.

'It's Willoughby!' Marianne shouted. She started to run towards him.

'No!' called Elinor. 'It's somebody different – oh!'

It was Edward Ferrars. He was on his way to visit them, but he seemed uncomfortable with them.

*It was Edward Ferrars. He was on his way to visit them,
but he seemed uncomfortable with them.*

'Have you just arrived?' Marianne asked him.

'No. I came two weeks ago,' he answered.

Two weeks ago! Why didn't he come to see Elinor then?

'Did you visit Norland?' Elinor asked.

And why were Edward and Elinor so cold together? Marianne asked herself. They were not like *real* lovers! Not like her and Willoughby!

'Yes, about a month ago.'

'How did it look?' Marianne asked him.

'Oh, as it always looks in autumn – plenty of dead leaves everywhere.'

'Those beautiful leaves!' Marianne said. 'Oh, I would love to see them again! Nobody there enjoys them!'

'Not everyone likes dead leaves,' said Elinor.

'Well then, Edward, do you like the beautiful hills here?' asked Marianne.

'Yes, but the roads at the bottom will get very dirty in winter.'

'How strange!' Marianne thought, and so did Elinor. What was wrong? She was unhappy about Edward's coldness, but she did not want to show her feelings.

Edward stayed at their house for a week, and was more friendly by the end of it. But there was still something different about him.

'Perhaps there's trouble with his mother,' Elinor thought.

'She wants me to be famous!' Edward told them once. 'But I only want some quiet, useful work. I'd like to be a priest and work for the Church.'

Elinor was not happy after his visit, but she worked busily in the house, and seemed calm.

One morning, Sir John arrived at their door, and invited them up to the house.

'Please come now!' he asked them. 'Come and meet two

12

beautiful young lady visitors! You'll like them so much! They're two sisters, relatives of Mrs Jennings . . .'

Miss Lucy Steele, the younger sister was really quite pretty. The older Miss Steele,★ was about thirty, and her face was neither sensible nor pretty. They were playing with Lady Middleton's children.

'John loves being a bad boy!' said Lady Middleton happily. Her oldest child took Miss Steele's handkerchief and threw it out of the window. 'And William is so playful!' William was now biting the lady's finger. 'Little Anna Maria,' continued Lady Middleton lovingly. 'She's always so quiet!' Just then, the little girl hit her head on the table and began to scream. The Miss Steeles gave her sweets and Lady Middleton took the crying child out of the room.

'What fine, clever children!' said Lucy Steele. 'I don't like very quiet children.'

'Quiet children can sometimes be very pleasant,' Elinor replied.

'Do you like Devon, Miss Dashwood?' said Miss Steele. 'Did you want to leave Norland? There were some handsome and amusing young men there, weren't there?'

'I'm sorry, but I really don't know,' said Elinor. She did not like the two sisters – Lucy Steele was not so free with her words as the older Miss Steele, but her face was not very honest. But the Miss Steeles liked the Miss Dashwoods, and Elinor and Marianne now had to spend an hour or two with them nearly every day.

During one dinner at Barton Park, Miss Steele said to Elinor 'It's very good news about your sister! Engaged so young and to a very handsome man! Perhaps you will be lucky too soon! Or perhaps you already have a special friend?'

★Jane Austen calls the older sister 'Miss Steele' and the younger 'Miss Lucy Steele'.

The secret escaped quickly from Sir John's lips.
'The letter F –,' he said.

The secret escaped quickly from Sir John's lips. 'The letter F —,' he said. 'That's a very important letter for Elinor!' Everybody laughed.

'But who is it?' Miss Steele asked.

'His name is Ferrars! And it's a great secret!' He spoke into her ear, but everybody could hear.

'Oh, what a nice young man!' said Miss Steele to Elinor. 'I know him very well.'

'Not *very* well,' Lucy said quickly. 'We saw him once or twice at my uncle's.'

'You know him?' Elinor asked. 'How interesting!'

But she could not find out anything more that evening. Then, a few days later, she and Lucy were walking in the park together.

'Do you know Mrs Ferrars?' Lucy asked suddenly. 'What kind of a woman is she?'

'Fanny's mother? No, I've never met her.'

'I want your advice — you see, maybe she will soon be a relative of mine.'

'Of yours?' Elinor said in surprise. 'Do you know her younger son then — Mr Robert Ferrars?'

'No,' Lucy said, 'no — I speak of Edward Ferrars, the older brother.'

Elinor could not speak, but her face changed colour.

'You're probably surprised,' Lucy continued, 'because it's a great secret. You see, we're engaged. Our engagement started four years ago.'

'And when did you meet?'

'Oh, we were only children then. Edward often stayed in my uncle's house.'

'I'm so surprised!' Elinor said. 'Are we talking about the *same* Mr Edward Ferrars?'

'Here — look! ' Lucy took a small picture from her pocket. It was Edward's face.

'You will keep my secret, won't you?' said Lucy. 'Only you can advise me! I love him so much, but his mother is a difficult woman – I'm not rich enough for her. Edward and I are so unhappy. We can't meet often, and we can only write letters about twice a year. What can we do?'

'I'm sorry,' Elinor said, 'but how can I help you?'

'His mother won't give him any money. He was very unhappy on his last visit to Barton, wasn't he? Didn't you notice?'

'Yes, we did.'

'Elinor, you seem cold! Have I said something wrong?'

'It's very difficult for you both, and I'm sorry for you.' Elinor tried to speak calmly.

'Must we break our engagement? Tell me, Elinor! Must we wait for years like this?'

'You have waited four years already.'

'If Edward gets some money, we *will* be happy, I know it! Can you ask your brother? Would he give Edward the job of priest in the church at Norland?'

Elinor felt sorry for Edward. Did he really love this young woman? 'Mr Ferrars is my friend,' she said, 'and I want to help him. But my brother won't listen to me.'

'Will you be in London this winter, Miss Dashwood?' Lucy asked.

'No, we can't possibly go,' Elinor replied.

'Oh, but I'd like to see you there. My sister and I are going to stay with some relatives. But of course, I'm really going there to see Edward – he's coming in February.'

Chapter 5   An Unkind Letter

Elinor was wrong about London. Mrs Jennings lived in London for part of each year, and she invited the two older Dashwood girls to visit her there in January. Mrs Dashwood agreed immediately.

'You two must go! Margaret and I will be very happy here together with our books and our music. Mrs Jennings is a kind and motherly sort of woman.'

'Mother, there is a problem –'

'Ah, my sensible Elinor sees a problem, of course!'

'She's a good woman, but not the politest –'

'Elinor, if you don't go, I will!' said Marianne. Marianne, of course, was hoping to see Willoughby in London. 'And you'll enjoy it too! Edward will be there.'

'Yes, you can meet his mother! She'll be your mother too, one day,' Mrs Dashwood said happily.

They arrived in London after a three-day journey in Mrs Jennings's carriage. Her house was large and comfortable. The girls had a very pleasant bedroom, and Elinor immediately began to write a letter. Marianne was writing too.

'I'm writing to Mother,' Elinor said, 'and so you need not write to her today.'

'I'm not writing to her!' said Marianne quickly.

'She's writing to Willoughby', thought Elinor.

Marianne finished the letter, and gave it to a servant to take. All evening, she listened for a knock at the door. At last there was a visitor – but it was only Colonel Brandon. Marianne ran out of the room.

'Is your sister ill?' he asked Elinor anxiously.

'Oh – no – she's just tired, and she has a headache,' Elinor told him. Poor man! she thought.

He talked politely for some time, and then asked her, 'Will you be pleased to have a new brother soon?'

'What do you mean?' asked Elinor.

He tried to smile. 'Well, everybody knows about Marianne's engagement.'

'I just want to know – have Willoughby and Marianne
agreed everything? Will they marry soon?'

'Everybody? That's not possible! Her family don't know about it – how can other people think this?'

'I'm sorry. I didn't mean to be rude. I just want to know – have Willoughby and Marianne agreed everything? Will they marry soon?'

Elinor could see his love for Marianne clearly, and so she tried to explain everything to him. It was better to be honest; there was not much hope for Colonel Brandon.

No other visitor came, and there were no letters for Marianne during the next few days. Marianne wrote another letter to Willoughby, but there was no reply.

'This is very strange,' Elinor thought. She decided to write home. Her mother *must* ask Marianne about the engagement.

A few days later, they all went to a party. It was a large party, with crowds of well-dressed people, and the room was very hot. Elinor found two chairs for them by the wall. Suddenly she saw Willoughby. He was standing near them, talking to a young lady.

Marianne saw him too. Light came into her face, and she jumped up. Elinor pulled her down again.

'Sit down! Be calm!' she ordered.

'Why doesn't he come and speak to me?' Marianne asked.

'Perhaps he hasn't seen you yet.'

Then Willoughby turned round and looked at them. He held out his hand – but to Elinor, not Marianne.

'Willoughby! What does this mean?' Marianne asked. 'Didn't you get my letters?'

He looked very uncomfortable. 'Yes, thank you. You kindly sent me news of your arrival.' Then he turned away to the young lady again.

Marianne's face was white now. 'Go to him, Elinor! He must explain! Surely there's some mistake!'

'No, my dear sister. It's not possible now. Wait until tomorrow.'

But the next morning early, Marianne was up and writing a letter. She was crying hard.

'Marianne, can I ask –?'

'No, Elinor, don't ask me anything. Soon you will know everything.'

Before lunch, a letter came – a reply from Willoughby. Marianne took it to her room, and Elinor followed. Her sister was lying on the bed, almost screaming in pain. Elinor took the letter and read it: 'I am sorry, but you must understand. I am engaged, and will soon get married. I do not want to hurt your feelings, but you have perhaps made a mistake. I did not mean to encourage you. My feelings for you were never those of a lover.'

'Oh, this is unkind!' Elinor said. 'This is not the letter of a gentleman!'

Mrs Jennings was waiting downstairs; she was planning to take them out.

'Ah, Marianne got a letter from Willoughby this morning!' she laughed. 'Poor Marianne looks quite ill with love! He must marry her soon!'

'Mrs Jennings,' Elinor said, 'they are not engaged!'

'Oh yes, my dear Elinor – it's not really a secret, is it? I tell everybody about it!'

Elinor told her the bad news. It was a very unpleasant surprise for Mrs Jennings, and she tried to do many kind things for Marianne all day. She brought her a glass of wine, gave her the best place by the fire, and cooked little bits of the nicest food for her. Marianne could not enjoy any of this.

'How can he do this, Elinor?' she said to her sister that evening in their bedroom.

'He's a bad man. If he breaks your engagement, it will be better finally. You'll see.'

'There was no engagement!'

Her sister was lying on the bed, almost screaming in pain.

'No engagement?' Elinor asked, surprised. 'But he loved you, didn't he?'

'Yes – no – he never said it. But he *seemed* to love me, and he encouraged me to love him, too. What has happened? Who is this woman? Oh, Elinor, you are so lucky! You can be happy – I can never be happy again!'

'Me, happy? Marianne, you don't know – and of course I can't be happy! Not when you are in so much pain.'

The next morning, Mrs Jennings brought them news about Willoughby's young lady. 'She is a Miss Grey, and very rich. And so he's broken his promise just for money!'

'Well, there was no real engagement between Willoughby and Marianne –'

'No, don't try to explain it. He's not a gentleman. But there's one good thing – Colonel Brandon can have her now. He'll be a very good husband! And he has a fine house at Delaford in Dorset with fruit trees in the garden – I'll encourage him at once! She'll soon forget about Willoughby.'

Colonel Brandon came to the house often, and was a good friend both to Elinor and Marianne. Marianne did not show any interest in him, but she was not unkind to him. She felt only her terrible pain. Soon Willoughby got married, and the news only made it worse. She wanted to leave London, but her mother didn't advise it. There was more to do in the city, Mrs Dashwood wrote in her letter, and their brother, John Dashwood, was coming to town soon. They must see him.

The Middletons were also in town. 'I shall never speak to Willoughby again!' Sir John said. Lady Middleton was polite, but a little cold, which was not unusual. In fact Elinor found this easier. Too many people were anxious about Marianne, and talked about her all the time.

And then the Miss Steeles arrived in London.

'You *are* in London, then!' Lucy said to Elinor. 'I thought so!'

Elinor understood her meaning very well, but said nothing.

Chapter 6   A Family Disagreement

Soon after this, their brother, Mr John Dashwood came to see them at Mrs Jennings's house. Colonel Brandon was there too that morning.

'And so you're all happy in your new little home at Barton! Edward told us all about it. I must meet the Middletons. Will you take me to meet them, Elinor?'

Elinor agreed. It was a fine day, and they could walk the short way to the Middletons' house.

'Colonel Brandon seems to be a good sort of man – a gentleman! Does he have money?'

'Yes, and a large house.'

'Wonderful! He'll be a good husband for you, Elinor!'

'For *me*?' Elinor asked in surprise.

'Oh yes! I watched him – he looked at you a lot!'

'No,' Elinor said, 'he doesn't want to marry me!'

'You're wrong, Elinor, wrong! You must try! You haven't got much money, it's true – but he'll have you, I'm sure! We'll all be very happy for you. Perhaps my sister and Fanny's brother will both marry at the same time!'

'What do you mean?' Elinor asked quickly. 'Is Edward going to marry someone?'

'We think so, yes, very soon. His mother has found the right young lady for him. Her name is Miss Morton, and she is very rich. And money is so useful – everything is very expensive now. We need more money for Norland.'

'Yes, John – but you're not poor.'

'Well, we're not rich! We're making a new flower garden, and of course we had to buy more furniture. Your mother took so

'What do you mean?' Elinor asked quickly. 'Is Edward
going to marry someone?'

much with her! Now, what is the matter with Marianne? She doesn't look well. She must be careful, if she wants to find a husband!'

Lady Middleton and Mrs John Dashwood were soon the best of friends. They were both selfish women. The Dashwoods invited the Middletons to dinner with Elinor, Marianne, Mrs Jennings, the Miss Steeles and Colonel Brandon. They invited Mrs Ferrars too.

'Oh, Elinor! I'm so anxious! Only you can understand this! I shall soon meet my new mother!' Lucy Steele said, entering the Dashwoods' house.

'Not yours, but Miss Morton's perhaps,' Elinor thought. Edward was not there – she was pleased. He was in London already, but could not come that evening.

Mrs Ferrars was a little, thin woman with a serious and quite unpleasant face. She did not say much, but looked at Elinor with dislike.

There were many servants, and the dinner was an expensive one. Later, in the sitting-room, John Dashwood showed one of Elinor's pictures to Colonel Brandon.

'How well Elinor paints!' he said. The Colonel agreed.

'Yes,' said Fanny, 'look, mother! Have you seen Miss Dashwood's picture?'

'Very pretty,' Mrs Ferrars said coldly, and did not look at it.

'It is a little like one of Miss Morton's pictures, isn't it?' Fanny continued.

'*She* paints beautifully,' Mrs Ferrars said, more warmly now. 'Miss Morton does everything well!'

Marianne didn't like this. 'Well, and who is this Miss Morton? And what does she matter? *Elinor* is here – we are talking about her, not Miss Morton!

Mrs Ferrars and Fanny were both very angry. But Colonel Brandon looked lovingly at Marianne. She put her arm round her sister and said quietly, 'Dear, dear Elinor! Don't be unhappy!' And then she began to cry.

'Ah, poor girl!' Mrs Jennings said.

'Poor Marianne,' her brother said to Colonel Brandon. 'She was quite beautiful a few months ago, but now it's all gone.'

Lucy Steele was very excited. She came to see Elinor the next morning.

'I'm so happy!' she said. 'Mrs Ferrars was so kind to me! Did you notice? Everything will be all right. I know it will!'

Marianne still didn't know anything about Edward's and Lucy's engagement. 'I must tell her soon,' Elinor thought.

The time for this came very quickly. One morning, Mrs Jennings hurried back into the house after her shopping.

'Have you heard the news?' she asked Elinor. 'Oh, it's so strange! Edward Ferrars and Lucy Steele are secretly engaged! And now Mrs Ferrars has heard about it! She is very, very angry. She has a rich young lady ready for Edward. Your sister Fanny shouted at Lucy, Lucy cried, and Mrs Ferrars has sent Edward out of the house! She is not going to give him any money – she's going to give it all to Robert!'

Robert, Edward's younger brother, was a well-dressed, but quite stupid young man.

'Lucy isn't rich! But she's my relative, and a nice young lady!' Mrs Jennings continued. 'Why can't they marry? Well, Edward is keeping his promise! He won't break the engagement – he has told his mother this. Poor young man! If he has no home, he can stay here!'

Elinor went to tell Marianne. 'How long ago did you hear about their engagement?' Marianne asked. She and Elinor were both crying now.

'Four months ago.'

'Four months! And you said nothing to me! All the time I was so unhappy and you were so kind to me! Oh, Elinor!'

'All the time I was so unhappy and you were so kind to me!
Oh, Elinor!'

'I wanted to say something, but it was a secret. And perhaps they will be happy together – I hope so.'

'How can you forget him so easily? Is your heart so hard?'

'Marianne, I do feel strongly for Edward. Yes, I loved him, and it was very painful. Fanny, Lucy and Mrs Ferrars have all hurt me too. But I couldn't say anything – I had to try to be calm, and to help you too. Please, Marianne, say nothing, and be polite to Lucy and Edward.'

Marianne kissed her sister warmly, and promised.

Chapter 7   All's Well That Ends Well

Marianne wanted to go home very much now, after two months in London. It was a long journey, quite difficult and expensive. But, luckily, Mrs Jennings offered them her help. Her other daughter, Charlotte, lived at Cleveland, only one day's journey from Barton, their home. Mrs Jennings wanted to visit her for Easter.

'We can travel there together,' she told the girls, 'and stay a few days. Then your mother can send her servant for you. Colonel Brandon is coming too. We shall have a happy time!'

'Oh no,' Marianne said to Elinor. 'I can't go there – Cleveland is in Somerset! Willoughby's home is near there.'

Elinor talked about their mother – 'We shall see her very soon!' and at last Marianne agreed.

But first Colonel Brandon came to see Elinor about Edward.

'I don't know Mr Ferrars well,' he said, 'but I met him a few times and liked him. He's going to be a priest, isn't he? Well, I can offer him work in my church at Delaford. The money is not much, and the house is quite small, but it's better than nothing. Will you tell him?'

Elinor was very surprised, but she agreed. That same morning, she took pen and paper, and began to write him a letter. Then suddenly the door opened, and Edward came in.

They both found it difficult to speak. 'You're leaving London,' he said. 'I wanted to say goodbye to you.'

Elinor explained the Colonel's offer to him.

'The Colonel has asked me to be his priest? Is it possible?'

'You still have friends – are you surprised?'

'No – you were always a good friend –'

'It is really Colonel Brandon's idea, not mine,' Elinor replied. 'But I'm very pleased about it.'

'I'll go and see him immediately!' Edward said, jumping up.

'And now he can marry Lucy,' thought Elinor sadly.

Elinor visited her brother for the last time in London.

'Has Colonel Brandon *really* given the job of priest to Edward?' he asked her. 'Why did he do that?'

'He wanted to help Mr Ferrars.'

'Well, Edward is a very lucky man! And now he will marry Lucy. But Mrs Ferrars mustn't hear about it!'

'Of course she'll hear about it!' Elinor said.

'Ah, but she'll be so unhappy! Edward is still her son!

'But she's forgotten that, hasn't she?'

'No, no – she is the most loving mother in the world!'

Elinor was silent.

'Possibly,' her brother continued, 'Mr *Robert* Ferrars will marry Miss Morton now.'

'Can't she choose?' asked Elinor. 'Or are Robert and Edward the same to her?'

'Of course it's the same thing! Robert will have all the money now.'

♦

Early on an April morning, they began their journey to Cleveland, and arrived there after three days. The house was large and modern, with beautiful trees round it.

Marianne enjoyed walking among the trees, thinking sadly of Willoughby, and his house only thirty miles away.

Marianne enjoyed walking among these trees, thinking sadly of Willoughby, and his house only thirty miles away. She walked through the wet grass and far away into the wilder part of the park. After four days, she caught a terrible cold.

At first, Elinor was not worried.

'Marianne must go to bed and sleep all night. Then she'll be better in the morning,' she told Colonel Brandon. He was much too anxious about her.

For a few days, it was just an ordinary cold. But then Marianne got much worse. She had a terrible headache and a fever, and began to say strange things.

'Is mother coming?' she asked anxiously. She lay heavily in her bed; it was about midnight. 'Oh, but if she goes round by London, I shan't see her! It's too far!'

Elinor sent for the doctor immediately. Her sister looked very ill. And who could go for their mother?

'I'll go,' said Colonel Brandon, and left at once.

Elinor sat with Marianne all night; the doctor didn't come until five o'clock in the morning.

'It's a dangerous fever,' he said. But he couldn't really help her. Everyone was very frightened now.

'She's a beautiful young girl!' Mrs Jennings cried. 'She can't die so young!'

Elinor tried to stay calm, but it was too much for her. The doctor came again.

'No, she's not better,' he said. Marianne was unnaturally quiet now, and sleeping heavily. 'Perhaps I can still help her – I'll give her some different pills.'

By about midday, Marianne was a little stronger, and the fever not so bad. By four o'clock, she was much better.

'She's out of danger now,' said the doctor, and Marianne began to sleep more comfortably.

Elinor ate some tea with Mrs Jennings, their first meal of the day. Then Mrs Jennings went up to bed. They were both very tired, but Elinor wanted to wait for her mother. She heard a carriage outside. But it was only eight o'clock – her mother and Colonel Brandon could not possibly arrive until ten. Who was it?

The door opened, and Willoughby walked in.

'I must talk to you, Miss Dashwood!'

'And I must *not* talk with you, Mr Willoughby!'

'Please! – it's very important, I've come all the way from London today!'

'Today?' said Elinor, surprised. 'Well then, sit down, and tell me your business at once. But please be quick!'

'How is your sister? Is the fever really better now? Your servant told me – is it true?'

'Yes, we hope it is.'

'And now, Miss Dashwood, am I a bad man or a stupid man? Bad – that's what you think, isn't it? But no, I'm not really bad, only stupid. And I'm very sorry – I want to tell you everything.'

He told her his story. He didn't mean to love Marianne. She was a pretty girl, and he amused himself with her at first. Then he started to love her seriously. He planned to marry her. But his old aunt, who lived near Barton, heard something terrible about him: he once took a young woman away from her husband, and then left her when she was having his baby.

'If this is true, Allenham House will never be yours!' she told Willoughby.

It was true; he had very little money, and was waiting for his aunt's house to be his.

'I have always spent a lot of money,' he told Elinor now. 'It's not good, I know. My happiest hours were with your sister, and I loved her, but I couldn't live without money. And so I decided to forget her, and to marry Miss Grey. My heart was hard then.

Then of course I saw you in London, and that was terrible! Marianne's sweet face – did you see the letter?'

'The letter that you wrote to her? Yes.'

'My wife wrote it. She found Marianne's letters, and was very angry. I held the pen, but they were all her words.'

'This is wrong!' Elinor said. 'Don't talk about your wife like that! You chose her – you chose all this!'

'My wife didn't love me then, and she doesn't love me now. I heard about Marianne's illness, and at once my love for her came back into my heart! I love only her! But she will never be mine now. Will you tell her all this? I hurt her badly, but I have also hurt myself. Am I still a very bad man? What do you think?'

'I'll tell her something. And I'm sorry for you, Mr Willoughby.' Perhaps he was not a very bad man, but he was a weak and selfish one, and he liked money too much.

Elinor sat thinking hard while she waited for her mother. At last Mrs Dashwood arrived with Colonel Brandon. She was very frightened, but Elinor quickly told her the good news that Marianne was better, and she ran upstairs to see her. She held her daughter in her arms, and offered to sit with her all night. Elinor was glad to agree; she needed to sleep now.

Her mother had something more to say the next morning. 'Elinor! Colonel Brandon opened his heart to me yesterday and told me about his love for Marianne. We were both in the carriage, and so frightened about her fever – it was natural to speak about our feelings for her! Oh, he is a good, unselfish man!'

'Yes,' Elinor replied, 'he is. If Marianne agrees to marry him, I'm sure they'll be very happy. What did you say to him?'

'I encouraged him – "You need time, just time, Colonel!" I told him. Marianne won't think about Willoughby for ever. Well, he's not so sure, but he's ready to wait. She'll be very near me at Delaford! The Colonel is not as handsome as Willoughby, but he's a much better man.'

'I love only her! But she will never be mine now.'

Every day now Marianne got a little better, and at last they were able to return to their house at Barton. Marianne was happy to be home again, but remembering everything was painful too. She went to her piano, and picked up some music. But it was a book of music with Willoughby's name in it, and she couldn't play.

'Well, Elinor,' she said. 'I'll be stronger soon, and then I shall study seriously. I shall read for six hours every day, and practise the piano. I'll learn a lot this way.'

Elinor smiled. One morning, she took Marianne out for a walk. Marianne looked up at the hill behind the house and said, 'I first saw Willoughby there. I can talk about it now – most of the pain has gone. But I *would* like to know – did he really love me? Or was it all a terrible mistake?'

Elinor told her about Willoughby's visit. Marianne turned white, but said, 'Thank you! oh thank you! It will be easier now!'

Soon Margaret returned from a visit, and Mrs Dashwood and her daughters were together again in their home.

Then, one day, one of the servants returned from the nearest town and said, 'Mr Ferrars is married. Did you know?'

Marianne began to cry, and Elinor looked terrible. Mrs Dashwood saw the pain on her face, and began to question the servant.

'Who told you this?'

'I saw Mr Ferrars and his new wife, Miss Lucy Steele. Their carriage stopped outside the hotel. Miss Steele – well, Mrs Ferrars now – told me. "I've changed my name!" she said. Mr Ferrars didn't say much.'

'Where were they going?'

'They came from London, and they were travelling west.'

'They're probably going to visit Lucy's uncle,' said Elinor quietly.

'She looked very well,' the servant continued, 'and very happy too. She's a handsome young woman!'

Elinor had no hope now. Before this day, there was always just a little hope. But now Edward was married – and so quickly, too! He wasn't a priest yet.

And then, through the window, they saw a man on a horse. Was it the Colonel? He was coming to visit them very soon. But, no! – it was Edward. Everyone saw, and waited silently. 'I *will* be calm,' Elinor told herself.

Edward looked white and anxious too, but Mrs Dashwood gave him her hand. 'We hope you will be very happy,' she said.

Elinor began to talk about the weather. Then she had nothing more to say, so Mrs Dashwood spoke again.

'Is Mrs Ferrars well? Is she with her uncle now?'

'She's well, thank you – but with her uncle?' He looked surprised. 'No, my mother is in London.'

'My mother is talking about Mrs *Edward* Ferrars,' said Elinor.

'Perhaps –' Edward said, 'perhaps you mean Mrs *Robert* Ferrars?'

'Mrs *Robert* Ferrars!' Marianne and her mother said together. But Elinor could not speak.

'Yes – my brother and Miss Lucy Steele are married now. Perhaps you haven't heard.'

Elinor jumped to her feet and ran out of the room.

Three hours later, she and Edward were engaged, and he was the happiest man in the world. He told her all about his engagement to Lucy.

'I was staying with her uncle some years ago,' he said, 'and I had nothing to do. I wanted to study, but I couldn't go to university for another year. And so I thought only about Lucy and her pretty face. We were much too young for an engagement. But I had to keep my promise.'

'But how did Lucy and Robert get married?' Elinor asked.

'Perhaps –' Edward said, 'perhaps you mean Mrs Robert Ferrars?'

'Robert went to talk to Lucy. "You can't marry Edward!" he told her. "It's very bad for the family!" He went to see her two or three times more – and you can guess the rest! He was pleased to take her from me. And I didn't have enough money for her. My mother is very angry with them, but Robert is still her favourite, and she'll give him something.'

Edward agreed to stay at their house for a week, and he and Elinor had some very happy days together. They talked about everything.

'But Edward,' she said, 'you were engaged to Lucy, and you spent a lot of time with me! Wasn't that wrong?'

'At first you were just a friend, but then I began to realize my feelings for you. Yes, it was dangerous – I had to leave, but I couldn't leave you at once,' he said.

Colonel Brandon arrived, and the two men were soon good friends. Edward would be the priest for the Colonel's village soon, but money was still a problem for him and Elinor. They did not need a lot, but they did need enough to live on.

Then John Dashwood wrote to her: 'Mrs Ferrars wants to see Edward again! She is ready to forgive him.'

'Yes, but she doesn't know about our engagement,' Edward said. Finally, he went to visit his mother. She was very glad to see him. Elinor was not as good as Miss Morton, but at last she agreed to his new engagement. She gave them enough money so that they could marry comfortably.

After the wedding, John Dashwood visited the happy pair in their new home. 'Well, dear sister,' he said. 'You *are* lucky, it's true. But I would prefer to have Colonel Brandon for my brother! He has a much better house! Perhaps Marianne – he doesn't love her yet, but maybe he will soon – you must encourage her, Elinor! Yes, you must encourage them both!'

Marianne was a very unusual girl. She loved a man when she was old enough to love him deeply. But she finally forgot him, and married another! She was nineteen then. And her new husband, Colonel Brandon, you will remember, was already 'an old man'! But they were very happy together, and Marianne soon loved him with all her heart.

Mrs Dashwood continued to live at Barton, but went to see her two daughters very often. They were, of course, living near their mother – Marianne in Delaford Park, and Elinor in the priest's house in the village. And Mrs Dashwood wasn't unhappy at home. Margaret was old enough to go to dances now, and her mother could think about a husband for her, too.

ACTIVITIES

Chapters 1–3

Before you read

1 Look at the pictures in this book. Which of these activities can you
   see in them? Write 'yes' or 'no' for each.

   a riding
   b swimming
   c reading
   d playing the piano
   e sleeping
   f carrying somebody
   g walking along the street
   h crying
   i greeting
   j sitting in a carriage

2 These words all come in this part of the story. Use a dictionary to
   check their meaning.

   advise anxious carriage encourage
   engaged gentleman sensibility servants

   Now choose the right meaning for each one from the list below:

   a a vehicle used before the age of cars
   b a polite, well educated man
   c worried and unsure
   d to tell somebody what you think they must do
   e to tell somebody that they are doing the right thing
   f promised in marriage
   g person employed to cook or clean in someone's home
   h full of sad or happy feelings

After you read

3 Who are these people?

   a a sensible girl aged nineteen
   b her brother's wife; she is rather rude
   c a large, happy woman who talks a lot
   d a sixteen-year-old girl who likes music
   e a quiet, sensible man of about thirty-five
   f a handsome young man who likes dancing

4 Answer these questions:
  a How does Marianne hurt her foot?
  b Who carries her home?
  c What interests does he share with Marianne?

Chapters 4–6

Before you read
  5 What do you think the title of the book means? How does the writer show 'sense' and 'sensibility' in the story? Discuss your ideas with other students.
  6 Choose the right answer.
  One of the young men wants to be a priest. A *priest* is:
    a a doctor of animals
    b a churchman
    c an adviser on the law

After you read
  7 Answer these questions:
    a Why is Marianne so deeply unhappy about the news in Willoughby's letter?
    b What do we know about his 'young lady'?
    c Which visitor often comes to Mrs Jennings's house to see the sisters?
  8 'You *are* in London, then,' Lucy says to Elinor. 'I thought so'. What deeper meaning does Elinor understand in these words?
  9 Why is Mrs Ferrars angry with Edward and how does she punish him?

Chapter 7

Before you read
  10 Choose the right answer.
  A *fever* means an illness with:
    a a high temperature
    b bad pains in the stomach
    c difficulty in sleeping

11 Work with a partner.

   Student A: You are Elinor. Ask Marianne why she is 'almost screaming with pain' over Willoughby's letter. Then try to give her sensible advice.

   Student B: You are Marianne. Tell Elinor about Willoughby's letter.

After you read

12 Who says these words? Who to?
   a 'I wanted to say goodbye to you.'
   b 'I love her. But she will never be mine now.'
   c 'You need time, just time.'
   d 'Did he really love me? Or was it all a terrible mistake?'

13 Answer these questions:
   a 'Elinor had no hope now.' Why not?
   b How do her feelings suddenly change?
   c Where do Elinor and Marianne live at the end of the story?

Writing

14 Which do you prefer to have as a friend: Colonel Brandon or Mr Willoughby? Say why.

15 You are Marianne. You met Willoughby for the first time yesterday. In your personal record book, describe what happened. Write about your feelings too.

16 Which people in this story are specially interested in money? Give examples of their interest. Are they good people or bad people?

17 Some people think that the writer's 'message' in this book is that strong feelings can be dangerous. Do you agree? Say why or why not.